CW01431708

Original title:

Topaz Murmurs Near the Witch Cradle

Copyright © 2025 Swan Charm

All rights reserved.

Author: Mirell Mesipuu

ISBN HARDBACK: 978-1-80559-249-5

ISBN PAPERBACK: 978-1-80559-748-3

Shadows Danced by Faerie Lights

In moonlit glades where whispers sigh,
Shadows waltz as fireflies fly.
Elves' laughter rings through the night air,
Magic lingers, shimmering fair.

A gentle breeze stirs the leaves low,
Guiding the paths where dreams do flow.
With twinkling stars above in sight,
The world awakens, pure delight.

Each corner turned, a tale untold,
Secrets by faerie folk unfold.
Cascading light upon the ground,
In every corner, wonder found.

Through soft moss beds where shadows creep,
The heart finds solace, secrets keep.
With echoes of laughter that entwine,
In faerie dances, we are divine.

Embrace the night, let go of fright,
For in this space, all feels so right.
In shadows danced by soft moon's glow,
Together we drift, and time moves slow.

Glimmering Paths to Arcane Realms

Beneath the stars, a path unfolds,
Glimmering trails of ancient bolds.
Winding through forests filled with dreams,
Where nothing is ever as it seems.

Whispers of magic beckon us near,
In silvered light, we shed our fear.
With every step, the air ignites,
Guiding us towards the mystical sights.

Crystals hum with a vibrant sound,
In this realm, our hearts unbound.
From glimmering shores to deep caves,
The journey calls, the spirit braves.

Songs of the ancients fill the air,
Each note a promise, a whispered prayer.
As shadows close, we forge our fate,
On paths of wonder, we await.

Ascend through mist, the stars a guide,
In arcane realms, our hopes reside.
Together we roam, forever free,
In glimmering paths, just you and me.

Cradle of Celestial Secrets

In twilight hues where dreams are spun,
Celestial secrets softly run.
Stars cradle wishes in their light,
As time surrenders to the night.

With every heartbeat, the cosmos hums,
A lullaby where starlight comes.
Hidden beneath the midnight sky,
Dreamers gather, hearts held high.

Galaxies whisper in secrets shared,
Through every pulse, the heart is bared.
In cosmic arms, we find our place,
A cradle of wonder, infinite grace.

The universe paints with colors bright,
In this stillness, we take our flight.
From nebulae to planets unknown,
In this cradle, love has grown.

So let our spirits take to flight,
With cosmic winds, we'll dance in light.
In the cradle of celestial skies,
Our dreams will shine where starlight flies.

Reverie of the Sunlit Silhouettes

In golden hues, the day awakes,
Where sunlit silhouettes take breaks.
Dancing shadows on the meadows sway,
In a gentle breeze, they find their play.

With every whisper of the trees,
Nature's chorus hums with ease.
Children laugh beneath the sun,
In moments fleeting, life's begun.

The horizon glows with colors bright,
As day transitions to soft twilight.
Each shadow tells a tale of old,
In reverie's grasp, our dreams unfold.

Beneath the arch of endless skies,
The heart awakens, spirit flies.
In sunlit rays, we find our place,
Within the warmth of nature's grace.

So let us gather, laugh and play,
In this reverie, we'll dance all day.
For in the light, our spirits mend,
In sunlit silhouettes, we transcend.

Whispers of Golden Twilight

The sun dips low, its golden hue,
A gentle breeze, an evening's cue.
Soft echoes dance on twilight's stage,
Nature's peace, the heart's true wage.

Rich colors blend, the world aglow,
Whispers of secrets only they know.
The dusk unfolds its velvet shroud,
As stars awaken, soft and proud.

In shadows cast by ancient trees,
A lullaby carried by the breeze.
Each whisper tells a tale of old,
Where dreams and memories softly mold.

With fleeting light, the moments sigh,
As night ascends, the day says goodbye.
In golden twilight, hearts align,
A fleeting dance, a sweet divine.

Echoes Beneath the Enchantress's Grove

Beneath the boughs where whispers weave,
Enchantress waits, her tales to leave.
The woodlands hum with secrets kept,
In shadows deep, the magic crept.

Moonbeams filter through leafy veils,
In every rustle, history trails.
The silence speaks, as hearts confide,
In the grove where dreams reside.

Secrets linger in the twilight air,
Soft laughter mingles with hope and care.
Where wishes bloom in silver light,
A guardian of the starry night.

Echoes dance among the trees,
Nature's whispers float like a breeze.
In the sacred hush, spirits play,
Beneath the enchantress, night turns to day.

Secrets in the Gilded Shadows

In shadows draped with golden seams,
Lies the heart of unsaid dreams.
Hidden paths of time unwound,
Where love's true essence can be found.

With every whisper, secrets spill,
Of fervent hopes and iron will.
Gilded rays of sunlit gold,
Hatch stories waiting to be told.

Beneath the oak, where silence reigns,
A tapestry of love remains.
Each glance shared, a spark ignites,
In gilded shadows, hearts take flight.

The world may fade, but truth will shine,
In the dance of fate, two souls align.
Through veils of twilight, they embrace,
Finding warmth in the hidden space.

The Alchemy of Silent Streams

Silent streams weave tales of old,
In whispers soft, the truth unfolds.
Rippling waters, secrets shared,
In their embrace, hearts are bared.

With every flow, a journey starts,
Carving through the land, through hearts.
Reflecting dreams in the moon's glow,
The alchemy of love can grow.

Gentle murmurs, the brook's sweet sigh,
Carrying wishes into the sky.
Each pebble holds a memory dear,
Mirrored dreams in waters clear.

As day breaks into vibrant hues,
The silent streams renew their muse.
Crafting moments in time's embrace,
Their magic flows in sacred space.

The Lament of Lost Lanterns

In the stillness of the night, they weep,
Flickering flames that silence keep.
Once bright paths in shadows dance,
Now they fade, a fleeting chance.

Echoes carry their silent cries,
From the ground to the starlit skies.
Memories lost in night's embrace,
Lanterns dim, a mournful trace.

They guide no more through paths unseen,
Once a light, now a ghostly sheen.
Each glowing spark, a tale once told,
A history in whispers bold.

Through winding roads where shadows play,
The lanterns drift, they slip away.
In the heart of dusk, they mourn,
A vibrant glow forever shorn.

For every flicker, a memory sways,
A dance of light in a darkened haze.
Yet in their loss, the stars remain,
A testament to joy and pain.

Silhouettes of Fable and Folklore

In the twilight, figures blur,
Whispered tales of 'was' and 'were'.
Myths that dwell in shadows' arms,
Echo softly their ancient charms.

Giants loom in thickets dense,
Wizards weave a shrouded sense.
Every creature, a tale to share,
Silhouettes linger on lonesome air.

The moonlight casts its silver thread,
Guiding seekers where dreams are fed.
In every crevice, stories dwell,
Waiting for hearts to weave their spell.

Winds carry secrets of days gone by,
Legends spoken in the sigh.
Through valleys deep where echoes soar,
We find the truth in folklore's core.

In the shadows, the night unfolds,
Revealing wonders yet untold.
Through fables bright, our spirits rise,
Silhouettes dance beneath the skies.

Wandering Whispers by the Altar of Time

In a realm where moments fade,
Whispers linger in twilight's shade.
Echoes of ages, softly chime,
Finding solace in the altar of time.

Footsteps trace a patterned path,
In the silence, we feel the past.
Every heartbeat tells a tale,
As memories wind like shadows pale.

Gentle murmurs weave through air,
Stories hidden, cherished rare.
Sifting sands that softly fall,
Whispers beckon, beckon all.

Each sigh a sigh of days long gone,
In this haven, we carry on.
Through the veil where fantasies roam,
We find our spirits calling home.

As the clock ticks, we hear it clear,
The echoes of what we hold dear.
Together we wander, hand in hand,
By the altar of time, we understand.

Chronicles in the Gloaming Whisper

When dusk descends on whispered dreams,
And the world dims by silver streams.
Tales begin in the gentle night,
Gloaming whispers take their flight.

In the corners of a fading light,
Grains of stories ignite the night.
Each twist a new enigmatic spin,
Chronicles of where we've been.

Moments caught in twilight's hold,
Fables woven, secrets told.
With every sigh, a chapter flows,
In the hush of dusk, our journey grows.

Heroes linger in shadows cast,
Echoes speak of the future past.
With every breath, we weave anew,
Chronicles old, and dreams pursue.

As stars awaken alongside the moon,
With every whisper, we find our tune.
In the gloaming, hearts find their clasp,
In every story, our souls grasp.

Enshrined in Starlit Histories

Whispers of ages dance in air,
Beneath the tapestry so bright.
Dreams of old in cosmic care,
Glimmering softly through the night.

Voices call from distant lands,
Echoes of love and of pain.
Within the sands, fate firmly stands,
Bound by the joys and the rain.

Each twinkling star, a story told,
Of lovers lost and battles fought.
In silence, secrets dare unfold,
In twilight's glow, all is wrought.

Paths of light weave through the dark,
Guiding souls where shadows fade.
A luminous journey leaves its mark,
As time's gentle hands invade.

Through celestial fields, we will roam,
Embracing shadows, light, and flight.
In starlit realms, we find our home,
Enshrined in histories of night.

Oracle's Breath Among the Trees

Branches sway with whispered lore,
A spirit dances in the breeze.
Mystic voices, ancient core,
Secret secrets held with ease.

Rustling leaves like heartbeats sound,
Foretelling futures yet untold.
In this haven, magic found,
Nature's wisdom, pure and bold.

Each brown trunk, a guardian wise,
Standing firm through storm and strife.
Glimmers of truth in emerald guise,
Breath of the forest, pulse of life.

Guided by the starlit night,
The oracle observes with grace.
Revealing paths to timeless light,
In every tree, a sacred space.

So share your dreams with rustling sighs,
Let intuition be your guide.
In nature's heart, where hope replies,
The oracle's breath shall abide.

Shadows of Moonlit Reverie

Silhouettes under silver beam,
Dancing softly, drawing near.
In the hush, we find our dream,
Soft whispers destined to appear.

Beneath the glow, secrets sway,
In shadows hid from daylight's glare.
A tender heart learns how to play,
In moonlit halls of fragrant air.

Time slows down, and moments blend,
Where fantasies and dreams entwine.
In this space, our worries mend,
Crafting tales from love divine.

So let us linger in the night,
Wrapped in warmth of silken sighs.
As whispers weave with soft delight,
In shadows deep, our yearning lies.

Awake, we drift in reverie's sea,
With dawn yet far on distant shore.
In moonlit arms, we're wild and free,
Citizens of a dream once more.

Echoes Weaving Through the Thicket

In tangled growth where secrets thrive,
Echoes murmur from the past.
Faint voices call, we feel alive,
Through the thicket's shadows cast.

Branches twist like memories held,
Entwined in nature's tender grasp.
Each rustle, every tale compelled,
In subtle moments, hope we clasp.

Paths obscure, yet hearts can see,
In the quiet, sparks ignite.
Weaving dreams like tapestry,
In the fading glow of light.

Nature's heart beats strong and clear,
Invoking courage to explore.
Through each thicket, we draw near,
Embracing echoes, evermore.

So let us wander, side by side,
In whispers of the tangled wood.
For in this journey, we abide,
In echoes woven, understood.

Luminescent Tides of Forgotten Echo

The moonlight dances on the sea,
Whispers of past, wild and free.
Waves crash softly on the shore,
Calling to hearts once more.

Ghostly ships with sails unfurled,
Haunt the dreams of many worlds.
Echoes of laughter, lost in time,
Binding the night with a silent rhyme.

Stars above in twilight's glow,
Guide the lost on paths below.
The tide rolls in, a gentle kiss,
Bringing memories wrapped in bliss.

Hearts once bold now softly sigh,
As shadows merge with the night sky.
In the depths where secrets lay,
The ocean sings of forgotten day.

So let us wander, hand in hand,
By luminescent tides on golden sand.
For in every wave that breaks anew,
Lives the heartbeat of me and you.

The Cauldron's Gentle Call

In the hearth, the fire glows,
A potion brews where mystery flows.
Herbs and whispers blend as one,
As dusk transforms into the fun.

The cauldron bubbles, secrets spilt,
Casting spells with winks of guilt.
Beneath the stars in twilight's grace,
Magic thrives in a cozy space.

Stir the mixture with heart and soul,
Let dreams and wishes play a role.
In the depths, the essence swirls,
A dance of fate, a world unfurls.

Gather around, good friends and kin,
Together we'll let the magic spin.
With laughter bright and tales of old,
The cauldron's call is a warmth to hold.

So raise a cup, let worries cease,
In this bubbling pot, we find our peace.
For in every drop, a story's spun,
Sealed with laughter, our hearts as one.

Dirge of the Glistening Woods

Amidst the trees, a silence lies,
Where olden secrets softly sighs.
A dappled light through branches weave,
In glistening woods, where spirits grieve.

The leaves, they tremble with a song,
Of tales forgotten, echoing long.
Footsteps whisper on the moss,
In nature's realm, we bear the loss.

Echoes of laughter fade away,
As shadows linger, night through day.
In every rustle, memories swell,
In silent woods, our lost farewell.

A dirge is sung by the gentle breeze,
Carrying whispers through the trees.
In the moon's pale gaze, we reflect,
On paths we've walked, our hearts connect.

So pause and listen, heed the call,
For in the woods, we're one and all.
In glistening shadows, we shall tread,
In harmony with the whispers of the dead.

The Alchemist's Song Beneath Summer Skies

Beneath the sun, where gold does gleam,
An alchemist dreams in a world of cream.
With potion and peddles in hand's embrace,
He bends the light to time and space.

Summer's warmth fuels his art,
Transforming atoms, a brand new start.
With every glance, the world shifts hue,
Creating wonders, old made new.

In the garden where time stands still,
He captures wishes with dreamer's will.
From petals bright to starlit sighs,
Each moment swirls 'neath open skies.

With laughter carried on soft winds' flight,
The alchemist smiles, all is right.
For in this song of life and grace,
He finds the dreams that time can trace.

So raise your hearts to summer's song,
In nature's arms, we all belong.
For beneath the vast and endless sky,
We are the dreams that never die.

Cobalt Dreams at Dusk's Embrace

Bathed in shades of twilight blue,
Whispers dance with shadows true.
Stars awaken, bright and bold,
Weaving tales of dusk untold.

Softly sings the evening breeze,
Kissing leaves on ancient trees.
Night unfolds its velvet shroud,
Wrapping dreams in visions loud.

Cobalt skies, a fleeting hue,
Promises of a night anew.
Guided by the moon's soft glow,
Hearts entwined in gentle flow.

Time suspends in quiet grace,
As the night unfolds its face.
Echoes of a distant past,
In cobalt dreams, to hold it fast.

Every star a spark of hope,
On this cosmic, endless slope.
Beneath the sky's vast, endless sea,
Dusk's embrace sets our spirits free.

Lurking Laughter from the Moonlit Glade

In the glade where shadows play,
Lurking laughter fades away.
Moonlight drapes a silver shawl,
Silencing the night's soft call.

Glimmers dance on leaves so bright,
Whispers weave through the night.
Crickets chirp a secret song,
Inviting all to join along.

Beneath the trees, the spirits sway,
Their laughter carries far away.
Echoes twirl through midnight air,
A symphony beyond compare.

In the silence, magic stirs,
As the night's enchantment purrs.
Every shadow holds a tale,
In laughter's echo, hearts set sail.

Beneath the gaze of the watchful moon,
The glade sings a haunting tune.
Lurking laughter, a playful tease,
In the night, we find our peace.

Resonance of Mystic Streams

Through the woods, the rivers flow,
Whispers soft, like secrets low.
Beneath the boughs, where shadows lie,
Mystic streams weave lullabies.

Ripples dance on waters clear,
Echoes drawing ever near.
Nature's music, pure and sweet,
In every pulse, our hearts repeat.

Flowing gently, tales unfold,
In the waters, dreams take hold.
Resonance of ages past,
A melody that's meant to last.

Every stone, a memory keeps,
As the river hums and leaps.
Reflection speaks in gentle tones,
Water's wisdom, lost in moans.

Underneath the sky's embrace,
Mystic streams, our sacred space.
In the flow, we lose our fear,
Resonance whispers, soft and clear.

The Enigma of Amber Breezes

Amber breezes softly sigh,
As the sun begins to die.
Floating whispers fill the air,
Carrying a fragrant prayer.

Through the fields, the echoes sing,
Of warmth and joy that autumn brings.
Mysteries in every gust,
In these winds, we place our trust.

Trees sway gently, shadows glide,
In this dance, our hearts abide.
Every leaf a story told,
In hues of amber and gold.

A gentle tug upon the soul,
As amber breezes take their toll.
Leaving traces, sweet and light,
On the canvas of the night.

Embrace the enigma's call,
In every rise, in every fall.
Amber breezes, fleeting grace,
In their warmth, we find our place.

Shadows of the Ancient Oracle

In caverns deep where secrets lie,
The oracles whisper, never shy.
Their shadows dance on ancient stone,
Guarding wisdom, forever known.

With every breath, the echoes call,
A glimpse of fate, a rise, a fall.
They weave the threads of time and fate,
In twilight's glow, we contemplate.

Beneath the stars, the seekers roam,
For answers held in silence, foam.
A flickering flame, a guiding light,
Through realms unseen, into the night.

The moonlight drapes on gnarled trees,
Whispers carried on the breeze.
In shadows cast, the truth will stir,
Unlocking worlds with every blur.

So listen close, ye who dare dream,
For in the dark, the oracles beam.
Their shadows twine with the pulse of time,
An ageless dance, a celestial rhyme.

Dusk's Precious Tapestry

As daylight fades to twilight's kiss,
The world transforms in gentle bliss.
A tapestry of hues unfurled,
Weaving stars into the world.

Lavender skies, and amber glow,
A fleeting beauty, soft and slow.
Whispers of night begin to play,
As dusk embraces the waning day.

The secrets sigh within the breeze,
Carried on the rustling leaves.
A moment caught in quiet grace,
In dusk's embrace, we find our place.

The moon ascends with silver light,
Casting dreams that dance in flight.
Each shadow spins a tale untold,
In the warmth of dusk, so bold.

So hold this time, so rich, so rare,
In every breath, the night we share.
For in this weave, life finds its song,
In dusk's embrace, where we belong.

The Orb of Enigma's Song

A crystal sphere of swirling night,
Its depths hold secrets, pure delight.
In flickers soft, the shadows blend,
Echoes of a time unpenned.

The world around in quiet thrall,
Each whispered thought becomes a call.
With open hearts, we seek to know,
The dance of fate in vibrant flow.

A melody of stars and dreams,
In soaring notes, the magic beams.
The orb reveals what's yet to come,
In its embrace, we all become.

A journey traced through realms unseen,
Each glimpse a thread in tapestry keen.
In twilight's glow, the truths unmask,
Revealing wonders, our hearts unask.

So dare to dream, to reach and find,
The orb of enigma, entwined with time.
Its song will guide through shadow's throng,
A symphony where we belong.

Murmurs of the Enchanted Hearth

In flickering light, coziness beckons,
Stories whispered, hearts it reckons.
The fire crackles with ancient tales,
While magic drifts on gentle gales.

Around the hearth, we gather near,
Each laugh and sigh, a bond held dear.
Embers glow with memories warm,
Wrapped in the night, safe from the storm.

The warmth of souls, rich as rich wine,
Each moment shared, a sacred line.
As shadows dance upon the wall,
We lean into the night's soft call.

With every whisper, the embers fade,
Transforming dreams in the warmth we've made.
In silent vows, our hopes ignite,
Under the stars, so pure, so bright.

So let the hearth sing its sweet refrain,
Of love and laughter, joy and pain.
In every murmur, we find our worth,
In the enchanted hearth, life's rebirth.

Enigma of the Wandering Spirits

Amidst the shadows, whispers call,
Lost souls drift where silence falls.
With secrets bound in midnight's haze,
They seek the light of distant days.

Through moonlit paths, they softly glide,
In dreams we wander, side by side.
Their laughter lingers, soft and sweet,
A haunting rhythm, heart's own beat.

Echoes of stories yet untold,
In every heartbeat, courage bold.
They dance on edges of the night,
In the enigma, find the light.

Life's fragile thread, a tapestry,
Interwoven with mystery.
As specters roam through time and space,
They leave a mark, an ancient trace.

In every sigh, the spirits breathe,
A timeless bond that weaves and weaves.
Together, lost, yet never far,
The wandering souls are who we are.

Ephemeral Dreams in Glass Bottles

In crystal prisons, visions gleam,
Like fleeting echoes of a dream.
Each shard reflects the moments lost,
Captured light, but at what cost?

With gentle hands, we hold them tight,
Yet, know they fade beyond our sight.
Like whispers brushed by autumn breeze,
They dance with time, and swiftly cease.

Each bottle holds a hopeful glance,
A chance to grasp a fleeting chance.
In fragile glass, our wishes soar,
But time, relentless, claims its score.

In midnight hours, we seek to find,
The bottled dreams that haunt the mind.
Though moments slip like grains of sand,
Their essence lingers, softly planned.

We drink the light, we taste the dawn,
In fragments lost, we carry on.
For every dream is worth the fight,
A whispered promise in the night.

The Serpent's Eye in Sun's Gaze

Beneath the heat, the serpent lies,
A glimmer bright in sunlit skies.
With emerald scales that weave and sway,
It beckons forth the light of day.

In shadows deep, it holds its sight,
A cunning glance that sparks the night.
While subtle whispers fill the air,
The serpent waits with patient care.

Its wisdom speaks in silent tones,
A dance of fate, a call of bones.
In every flicker of its eye,
Lies ancient truth and whispered lie.

As sun descends, the shadows creep,
The serpent stirs from whispered sleep.
With every twist, it shapes our dreams,
In golden rays, reality beams.

Embrace its charm, for all it hides,
In every turn, adventure bides.
The serpent's eye in sun's embrace,
Reveals the truths we strive to face.

Flickers of Enchanted Memory

In twilight glimmers, pasts unfold,
Forgotten stories etched in gold.
Each flicker sparks a distant place,
Where laughter echoed, time's embrace.

Through golden fields where shadows play,
We weave our dreams in soft ballet.
In every sigh, a memory stirs,
Awakens tales that time obscures.

With whispers sweet, they softly call,
The echoes linger, rise and fall.
A tapestry of joys and tears,
We gather close, dispel our fears.

As fireflies dance in evening's glow,
The magic stirs, a gentle flow.
In every heartbeat, love survives,
The spark that keeps our dreams alive.

Embrace the past, let it ignite,
The flickers of enchanted light.
In memories, we find our thread,
A woven path where hearts are led.

Secrets Among the Shimmering Stones

In the quiet of the night, they gleam,
Mysterious whispers in the stream.
Each glint holds a tale, ancient and wise,
Guarded by shadows under the skies.

Beneath the moon's soft, silver touch,
Silence cradles secrets, oh so much.
The stones know stories, lost with time,
Riddles entwined in rhythm and rhyme.

Caught in the web of nature's bliss,
Every glimmer recalls a sweet kiss.
Underneath stars, they twinkle and sigh,
Echoes of dreams that time can't deny.

In the realm where darkness meets light,
The stones share whispers, ever so bright.
With each breath of wind, their secrets play,
Guiding the heart on its wandering way.

They call to those who seek and yearn,
In their silence, many lessons to learn.
Among the shimmering stones we stand,
Holding the secrets of this ancient land.

Heartbeats of Solstice Shadows

When the sun dips low, shadows arise,
Softly weaving stories 'neath twilight skies.
The solstice hums a gentle tune,
A dance of whispers beneath the moon.

Fingers of dusk stretch long and thin,
Painting the night where dreams begin.
Each heartbeat thunders in the still air,
Time stands still as hearts lay bare.

Embers flicker, a warmth remains,
The echo of laughter, the pulse of refrains.
In this quiet, the universe sways,
Stirring the magic of lingering days.

The stars play tricks, a celestial show,
Guiding lost souls as they come and go.
Among the shadows, moments collide,
A tapestry of heartbeats, wild and untied.

As night enshrouds the world in peace,
In every heartbeat, a sweet release.
The solstice shadows breathe and inspire,
Igniting dreams with their rapturous fire.

Enchanted Stories in Candlelit Glades

In glades where the softest breezes sigh,
Candlelight flickers like stars in the sky.
Each glow a secret, a tale to unfold,
Whispers of magic in the night, bold.

Lost in the shimmer of soft waxed light,
Creatures of dreams dance, hearts take flight.
The stories weave through the fragrant air,
Creating a lullaby, tender and rare.

A flickering flame tells of long-forgotten lore,
Echoes of laughter shimmer on the floor.
In every glow, a promise resides,
Of love and adventure where wonder hides.

Among the shadows, mysteries beckon,
In this glade of magic, hearts can reckon.
Each candle's flame is a story untold,
Illuminating paths to treasures of old.

As night deepens, the tales come alive,
In enchanted glades, hopes glide and thrive.
With every flicker, the world ignites,
Bringing forth dreams into the starry nights.

Glowing Echoes of the Nightingale

In the gentle dusk, a melody flows,
The nightingale sings where the wild rose grows.
Each note a whisper, sweet and divine,
Carrying secrets in the moonlit vine.

Through the thickets, her song takes flight,
Painting the dark with notes of light.
Melodies dance on the edge of sleep,
In the tranquil night, the heart will keep.

With glowing echoes that ripple and weave,
The nightingale sings the stories weieve.
From joyful springs to sorrowful tales,
Her voice enchants like the softest gales.

In the embrace of night, we lose all time,
Every heartbeat follows her tender rhyme.
In the symphony of stars, we catch our dreams,
Held close by the glow of her silver beams.

As dawn approaches, the echoes delay,
Lingering soft in the break of day.
For the nightingale's song will forever remain,
A glowing reminder, love's beautiful pain.

Potion of Celestial Whispers

In a bottle of glass, soft whispers dwell,
Brewing starlight, casting a spell.
Moonlit dreams in a silken haze,
Fragrant echoes of twilight's gaze.

Flickering shadows dance in the night,
Colors swirling, gentle and bright.
The essence of hope in each tiny drop,
A melody rising, never to stop.

Breathe in the magic, let it unfold,
Tales of the cosmos in secrets told.
In every sip, a universe flows,
A treasure of wonders, gently bestows.

Embrace the silence, hear the stars sing,
With each heartbeat, the heavens take wing.
Grounded in earth, yet soaring above,
Wrapped in the warmth of celestial love.

Mysteries shimmer in the soft light,
Nurtured by dreams that linger at night.
The potion whispers of worlds unseen,
Inviting the brave to where they have been.

The Glimmering Oracle's Call

In a forest dense, where shadows play,
The oracle waits, in twilight's gray.
Voices of ancients, soft yet bold,
Secrets of futures and tales of old.

Glimmers of wisdom in a silver stream,
Reflecting the essence of every dream.
In the rustling leaves, whispers arise,
The heart seeks answers in starlit skies.

With every breath, the air shimmers bright,
Mysteries wrapped in the folds of night.
Paths intertwine, as fates are drawn,
Under the gaze of a new dawn.

Echoes of laughter, shadows of tears,
The oracle sees through all of our fears.
Trust in the vision, the journey ahead,
In the realm of the mystic, where few dare tread.

Step forth with courage, embrace the call,
In the heart of the forest, the cosmos will fall.
Glimmers of guidance, soft as a sigh,
The oracle whispers, beneath the vast sky.

Secrets in the Veiled Thicket

Hidden away in the green embrace,
Where sunlight dances and shadows trace.
Secrets unfurl, like petals in bloom,
In the heart of the thicket, life finds room.

Whispers of creatures, soft and low,
Echoes of stories that linger and flow.
Veiled in the mist, the past comes alive,
Among tangled branches, memories thrive.

A world of wonder beneath leafy canopies,
Silent songs carried by the gentle breeze.
Each rustle and murmur, a tale to be spun,
In the thicket of dreams, where all has begun.

Step lightly, dear wanderer, speak to the trees,
In their ancient wisdom, the heart finds ease.
Paths less traveled hold treasures untold,
In the secrets of silence, courage grows bold.

As twilight descends, the magic takes hold,
With stars as your guide, let your spirit be bold.
For in the veiled thicket, mysteries thrive,
A sanctuary where dreams come alive.

Chlorine and Gold Under Velvet Skies

By the shimmering pool, the moonlight glows,
Chlorine and gold in a dance that flows.
Ripples of laughter under starry light,
A canvas of dreams in the quiet night.

The water reflects moments, sweet and rare,
Soft whispers of love linger in the air.
Diving into memories, so vivid and bold,
As stories unfold, like threads of gold.

Friends gather close, bathed in the glow,
Each splash a reminder of days we know.
Veils of nostalgia wrap us in grace,
As laughter and memories fill up the space.

Beneath velvet skies, the constellations gleam,
Every star a promise, every wish a dream.
Time may be fleeting, but moments stay strong,
In the heart of the night, we all belong.

So let us cherish this night ever bright,
With chlorine and gold, our spirits take flight.
Under the vast heavens, together we stand,
In the warmth of our bonds, forever hand in hand.

Whispers of Golden Dawn

The morning light begins to play,
Soft hues of gold greet the day.
Birds sing sweetly in the trees,
A gentle breeze stirs the leaves.

As shadows fade, the sun will rise,
Painting colors in the skies.
Nature wakes from slumber deep,
In its arms, the world will leap.

The flowers bloom, a vibrant sight,
With petals kissed by morning light.
Whispers dance upon the air,
Promises made without a care.

In the warmth of golden hour,
No heart can doubt its magic power.
A symphony of life unfolds,
In every story the dawn holds.

Let each heart embrace the morn,
For in its light, we are reborn.
In the whispers of the day,
All our worries fade away.

Secrets Beneath the Moonlit Glade

In the glade where shadows weave,
Ancient tales the night could cleave.
Moonlight spills on leaves aglow,
Secrets dance in silvery flow.

A gentle hush, the world at rest,
Nature's pulse within the chest.
Stars peek through the evergreen,
Whispered thoughts that remain unseen.

The owls hoot, a mystic sound,
Echoes deeply through the ground.
Every rustle, every sigh,
Tells of dreams that won't run dry.

Beneath the moon's enchanting gaze,
Hearts intertwine in twilight's blaze.
A tapestry of night unfurls,
Binding souls in hidden swirls.

In this realm where shadows play,
Magic lingers, come what may.
Secrets shared without a fear,
In the moonlit glade, they're near.

The Enchantment of Amber Shadows

In the woods where shadows blend,
Amber light begins to send.
With twinkling fires flaring bright,
Whispers echo through the night.

Each tree stands tall, a sentinel,
Guarding stories it won't tell.
Leaves aglow in warm embrace,
Nature dances with such grace.

Golden hues spread far and wide,
Every corner, a secret guide.
Footsteps soft on mossy ground,
In the silence, wonders found.

As twilight weaves its magic thread,
Echoes linger where we tread.
Dreams come alive, entwined in glow,
In amber shades, our spirits flow.

Where light and dark so often meet,
Mysteries connect, bittersweet.
In the heart of this enchanted place,
We find solace, we find grace.

Echoes in the Forgotten Grove

Deep within the forgotten grove,
Echoes of memories softly rove.
Whispered secrets through the trees,
Carried gently on the breeze.

Time stands still in this embrace,
Nature holds a sacred space.
Footsteps lost on winding ways,
Guide us through forgotten days.

Each rustling leaf, a tale untold,
Of lives once lived and dreams of old.
In the twilight's tender light,
Shadows dance, flickering bright.

Among the roots where spirits lean,
In silence, whispers can be seen.
The past and present intertwine,
In the grove, a sacred sign.

Let us wander, heart in hand,
Through this old and timeless land.
In echoes found beneath the boughs,
We honor all who made their vows.

Mystical Hues of Evening's Embrace

Whispers of twilight softly flow,
Painting the sky with a violet glow.
Stars begin their distant dance,
Cradled in night's gentle trance.

The moon, a sentinel so bright,
Guides the dreams into the night.
Clouds like brushes, stroke the air,
Veils of mystery everywhere.

Crickets serenade the closing day,
As shadows waltz in their silent sway.
Soft breezes blend, a lover's sigh,
In the embrace of the evening sky.

Colors merge, a watercolor stream,
Where the heart can dare to dream.
Lost in hues of purple and gold,
Tales of the night softly unfold.

In this realm of tranquil grace,
Time stands still in a warm embrace.
As darkness deepens, hope provides,
A canvas where the soul resides.

Flickers of Light in the Darkened Glen

Beneath the boughs where shadows play,
Flickers of light dance and sway.
Fireflies weave tales of the night,
Bringing magic, pure delight.

Misty coolness wraps the trees,
Rustling softly with the breeze.
Whispers linger in the air,
Secrets of the woods laid bare.

In the darkened glen, time slows,
As luminous points rise and glows.
Paths illuminated by a spark,
Leading wanderers through the dark.

Nature hums a soothing tune,
Underneath the watchful moon.
Every flicker tells a story,
Chasing shadows, seeking glory.

With each breath, a promise clear,
In this haven, free from fear.
Flickers of hope that guide the way,
In the heart of the night's ballet.

Tales from the Enchanted Hollow

In the hollow where magic reigns,
Whispers of old charm remains.
Trees wear cloaks of emerald leaves,
Cradling secrets nature weaves.

Mystical creatures hide and sigh,
Underneath the starlit sky.
With every rustle, every sound,
A tapestry of dreams is found.

Brooks babble soft melodies,
Flowing gently 'neath ancient trees.
Moonbeams glisten on the ground,
Echoes of laughter all around.

In the heart of this sacred space,
Time dances with a slower pace.
Stories etched in winds that roam,
In this enchanted place called home.

Tales of wonder, love, and strife,
Weave the fabric of true life.
Explore the hollow, lose control,
And let its magic soothe the soul.

Serpentines of Silence and Stars

Winding paths through the quiet night,
Stars above, twinkling bright.
Silence wraps the world in peace,
Inviting minds and hearts to cease.

Each step a whisper on the ground,
In the hush where dreams are found.
Gathering shadows, holding time,
As the gentle night begins to chime.

Secrets hide in every corner,
Stories linger, ever warmer.
Serpentines lead us, far and wide,
On a journey where hopes abide.

Feel the cool breath of the night,
Guiding souls with soft delight.
In the silence, find your star,
Illuminating just who you are.

So wander deep where whispers start,
Embrace the calm within your heart.
Let the serpentines of this night,
Carry your dreams to dazzling heights.

Emerald Veils Over Forgotten Tales

In forests deep where shadows play,
Emerald veils dance night and day.
Whispers from the ancient trees,
Carry secrets on the breeze.

Forgotten tales in twilight's glow,
Echo through the earth below.
Beneath the moss, the stories sleep,
Guarded by the spirits deep.

Time holds tight to nature's grace,
Each leaf hides a memory's trace.
Crickets sing their lullabies,
While the moonlight softly sighs.

The brook flows by with gentle ease,
Cradling dreams like autumn leaves.
Emerald veils weave in the night,
Wrapping tales in silver light.

Awaken now, dear wanderer bold,
Seek the wonders yet untold.
For in this realm where magic thrives,
Forgotten tales come back alive.

Spellbound in the Silver Mist

In the hush of night so deep,
Dreams are caught, but never sleep.
Silver mist wraps hearts in sighs,
Magic dances, softly lies.

Each breath taken, a spell cast,
Moments linger, shadows vast.
Whispers linger, soft and sweet,
Where the earth and dreamers meet.

Moonlit paths hold stories rare,
While stars twinkle with silent care.
Enchanting echoes draw us near,
Magic spun from every tear.

Through the fog, the night unfolds,
Tales of love and courage told.
Hearts entwined in silver threads,
A spellbound world where no one dreads.

Raise your voice to those above,
Seek your dreams, and find your love.
For in this mist, all hopes are found,
A magic realm, forever bound.

Curls of Twilight in Brewed Potions

In cauldrons deep, the twilight brews,
Curls of magic in swirling hues.
Whispers of herbs and moonlit skies,
Secrets linger as the potion dries.

With every stir, the shadows swell,
Echoes of stories they won't tell.
A pinch of starlight, a dash of dreams,
A dance of fate in silver streams.

Through crystalline vials, fate is laid,
Curls of twilight in charms displayed.
Brewed with care, where wishes soar,
Potion-casts on the heart's door.

As night descends, the elixirs gleam,
Filling the world with a wistful dream.
Curls of time in every sip,
Journey forth on magic's ship.

Raise your chalice, take a chance,
Join the twilight's secret dance.
For in these brews, adventure waits,
In twilight curls, unlock your fates.

Vows of the Wandering Spirits

In moonlit haze, the spirits roam,
Finding peace, they wander home.
Vows exchanged in whispered night,
Binding hearts in ethereal light.

With every call, a promise made,
Through time and space, their love won't fade.
Wandering souls, forever free,
Bound by dreams, like waves at sea.

In ancient woods where shadows breathe,
Each step holds what we believe.
Vows encircle in a gentle breeze,
Echoing soft beneath the trees.

Through the night, their laughter sings,
A chorus born on silver wings.
Awakened hearts feel no despair,
For love's essence lingers there.

Wandering spirits, hear their calls,
Through timeless woods, the magic falls.
In every vow, a thread of fate,
Binding dreams before it's late.

Whispers of Forgotten Realms

In shadows cast by ancient trees,
The whispers dance on evening breeze.
Stories told by silken night,
Echo softly, out of sight.

Lost in time, where secrets dwell,
In every stone, a crafted spell.
Breath of legends, faint and rare,
Awakens dreams upon the air.

Through tangled paths, the spirits sigh,
Guiding hearts, they will not die.
In gentle tones, their voices call,
From hidden glades, they seek to enthrall.

Around the fires, we gather near,
To hear the tales, to feel the fear.
A tapestry of fate and lore,
Woven tightly, forevermore.

In every glance, a memory glows,
Of distant realms that time bestows.
With every breath, a promise made,
In the whispers, we are remade.

The Lure of Glittering Waters

Beneath the sun, the waters gleam,
Caught in the light, a silken dream.
Ripples dance like laughing sprites,
Inviting souls to summer nights.

Fish dart quickly, shadows play,
Beneath the waves, they drift away.
The surface sparkles, life runs deep,
A hidden realm where secrets sleep.

Can you hear the sirens' song?
Pulling hearts where they belong.
With every splash, a tale unfolds,
Of treasures lost and dreams of gold.

The shoreline whispers soft and sweet,
Where earth and water gently meet.
Each wave a promise, rising high,
To kiss the sky and wander nigh.

As twilight drapes its velvet veil,
The glitter beckons with its trail.
In moonlit dances, fate aligns,
Forever drawn by water's signs.

Echoing Lullabies in the Gloom

In the stillness, a soft refrain,
Lullabies whisper through the rain.
Echoes linger down the lane,
Carried softly, sweet yet plain.

The shadows weave their gentle forms,
Telling tales of gentle storms.
Each note a breath of dreams defined,
A comfort for the weary mind.

Underneath the starlit dome,
Hearts find solace, finding home.
A serenade of soft embrace,
Guiding thoughts to a tranquil place.

Through the darkness, shadows play,
Shimmering hints of night and day.
With tender notes, they fill the air,
A gentle balm for every care.

In this lullaby, fear fades away,
Time slows down, we choose to stay.
Wrapped in dreams, we find our tune,
Beneath the watchful, silver moon.

Glistening Heartbeats Beneath the Boughs

Amidst the leaves, a rhythm beats,
In every pulse, the forest greets.
Beneath the boughs, where life unfolds,
A symphony of stories told.

The sunlight filters, dappling light,
A dance of shadows, twirls of white.
Each heartbeat echoes nature's song,
In this embrace, we all belong.

Whispers in the rustling leaves,
Tales of joy that nature weaves.
Among the roots, where spirits thrive,
In every moment, we feel alive.

Through tranquil paths, we wander free,
In the heartbeat of the verdant sea.
Together here, we find our peace,
As heartbeats guide, our troubles cease.

As twilight paints the sky with grace,
We linger here, a sacred space.
In glistening whispers, all is well,
Beneath the boughs, where we can dwell.

Radiance Encircles the Witching Hour

In shadows deep the candles glow,
Whispers dance where secrets flow.
The moonlight casts a silver hue,
While dreams unravel, old and new.

Stars adorn the velvet sky,
A tapestry as night birds fly.
With each tick the world holds breath,
As magic stirs, defying death.

Mysteries bloom in fragrant air,
Echoes linger, soft and rare.
The hour sways, a timeless waltz,
In every heart, a gentle pulse.

Veils are lifted, truths laid bare,
In the silence, we all share.
The witching time, a sacred space,
Where every soul can find its grace.

With every thought, connections spark,
A universe ignited in the dark.
Joyful laughter, and silent tears,
In this hour, we conquer fears.

Harmonics of Hidden Realms

In echoing woods where shadows creep,
The harmonics of dreams run deep.
Each rustle speaks of tales untold,
In whispered notes of silver and gold.

Fingers trace the glowing stream,
While the unseen weaves through our dream.
Melodies sway on the breeze,
Calling forth the ancient trees.

Step lightly through the hidden glade,
Where time and space in silence fade.
Notes of nature begin to sing,
Awakening all forgotten things.

With every turn a story unfolds,
In vibrant hues, life's dance beholds.
A symphony beyond our sight,
Resonates in the heart of night.

So listen close, let go of fear,
The unseen world is drawing near.
In harmonics, let us unite,
As magic blooms beneath the night.

Nightingale's Promise Over Twilight Streams

Under the veil of twilight's gleam,
A nightingale sings the sweetest dream.
Notes cascade like silver streams,
Flowing softly, weaving themes.

The water glistens, the stars ignite,
Every ripple dances in the night.
Promises whispered through the trees,
Carried gently on the breeze.

Each melody a heart's embrace,
Softly echoing time and place.
The world pauses, breath held tight,
In the beauty of fading light.

Beneath the sky, where shadows blend,
A song of hope seems never to end.
In twilight's arms we find our way,
Guided by a tune that stays.

With every note, a wish takes flight,
In the soft embrace of fading light.
As nightingale calls, we join the song,
In unity, we all belong.

Echoes of the Ineffable Grove

Whispers travel through ancient trees,
Crafted softly by the breeze.
In the grove where shadows play,
Echoes speak in a timeless way.

Figments of light in the dappled shade,
Underneath the life that's made.
Each pulse a heartbeat of the ground,
In this realm, magic is found.

Winding paths through thickened green,
Where secrets linger, and dreams convene.
The air is thick with stories old,
In this refuge, wisdom unfolds.

With every step, the silence sings,
Revealing all that nature brings.
An ineffable dance of life and fate,
In this grove, we contemplate.

So close your eyes and breathe it in,
The echoes of where life begins.
In this sacred space, be free to roam,
For in the grove, we find our home.

Haunting Harmonies of the Nightshade

In the depths where shadows play,
Whispers weave through night's ballet.
Moonlight dances on the ground,
Echoes of a lost sound.

Faintly sung by winds that sigh,
Secrets spun beneath the sky.
Glimmers found in darkened lanes,
Bound to night like fleeting chains.

Crimson blooms of dusk's embrace,
Linger in this hollow place.
Bitter sweet and bittersweet,
Fading echoes in retreat.

Stars descend like silent prayer,
Brushing gently through the air.
Haunting notes of memory,
Sonic threads that pulse with glee.

With the dawn, the tales would shift,
Yet in dreams, the shadows drift.
Harmonies of nightshade grow,
In the heart, they linger slow.

Cradle of Dreams in Verdant Woods

Beneath the boughs, where shadows hum,
A cradle soft, where dreams can come.
Whispers dance through leaves of green,
Nature's breath, a gentle sheen.

Each petal sighs in soft delight,
Frogs croon songs to the moonlight.
Cool streams murmur their secrets low,
Footsteps traced where wildflowers grow.

In this haven, spirits play,
Chasing echoes of the day.
Twilight weaves its silken thread,
Among the trees, and dreams are bred.

While night descends on vibrant ground,
In soft silence, joy is found.
Cradled deep in nature's grasp,
Time unravels, dreams en masse.

Nocturnal whispers wake the night,
Tender feelings, pure and light.
In verdant woods, all hearts align,
Nestled close, where stars brightly shine.

The Allure of Starlit Silences

In the realm of starlit shades,
Silence weaves its soft cascades.
Velvet skies, a painter's muse,
Glimmers where the heart can fuse.

Breathless moments, time stands still,
As the cosmos bends to thrill.
Fingers trace the light above,
In this space, the whispers love.

Each twinkle holds a secret bright,
In the dance of endless night.
Here, the shadows do not weep,
Promises that dreamers keep.

A canvas vast, where wishes soar,
Underneath the universal lore.
Night unveils her tender charms,
Closing softly in her arms.

From starlit depths, the silence sings,
Wrapped in warmth, the peace it brings.
In the quiet, hearts confess,
To the allure of night's caress.

Echoes of Enchantment in the Ether

Vibrations sway in realms unseen,
Echoes dance where hopes have been.
Mystic sounds on breezes sail,
Carried forth by twilight's veil.

A tapestry of whispers weave,
Through the air, they softly grieve.
Crystalline notes that swirl and twine,
Bringing forth a dream divine.

In this realm of airy light,
Magic pulses, holding tight.
Each echo tells a tale of old,
Where secrets waiting to unfold.

Breath of stars in silent grace,
Cascading dreams through time and space.
Enchantments flow like rivers wide,
In the ether, spirits glide.

Within these echoes, find your muse,
Awakening the heart's deep views.
In connection pure and sweet,
Every whisper feels complete.

A Symphony of Shards and Whispers

In twilight's hush, the echoes play,
Soft whispers dance in shadowed sway.
Fragments of light, like crystal dreams,
Compose a song of silent beams.

Through tangled woods, the voices weave,
Each note a story, dusk's reprieve.
A melody calls from hidden depths,
Where silence dwells and wonder crests.

Shards of laughter, tears like rain,
In every moment, joy and pain.
The heart beats steady, time unwinds,
In symphonies of open minds.

The starlit skies, a canvas vast,
Reflecting dreams of every past.
A serenade for souls awake,
In harmony, the silence breaks.

So listen close, let spirits soar,
In shards and whispers, find your core.
The night reveals what light hides tight,
A symphony of love, of light.

Gospel of the Unseen Cascade

Beneath the veil of timeless flow,
An unseen cascade starts to grow.
Whispers of water, truth and grace,
Reveal a world we long to face.

With every droplet, secrets blend,
Nature's gospel, a gentle mend.
In valleys deep, where shadows lie,
The stories of the earth will sigh.

Through rocky paths, the current sings,
Of ancient tales and hidden springs.
In every ripple, life unfolds,
A testament to dreams retold.

The trees will sway, the flowers bloom,
A mystery wrapped in nature's loom.
In silent moments, hearts will learn,
The cascade's wisdom, tides that turn.

So gather close, let waters guide,
In the gospel, let love abide.
For every flow has much to share,
From unseen depths to open air.

Mothlight Trails to Serpent's Heart

In realms where shadows softly dwell,
Mothlight trails weave stories to tell.
Guided by glimmers, paths ignite,
To the serpent's heart, hidden from sight.

With every flutter, a whisper calls,
Through tangled thorns, where twilight falls.
Secrets linger in the night air,
A journey worn with tales of care.

The silver beams, like dreams released,
Lead fearless souls to find their feast.
Ensnared by wonder, hearts drawn near,
To grasp the truths we hold most dear.

The serpent coils with ancient grace,
A guardian's touch in a sacred space.
With mothlight leads, we take our chance,
In the dance of fate, a timeless dance.

So heed the trails that spark with light,
For each will guide us through the night.
And in the heart of secrets curled,
Awaits the beauty of our world.

The Lantern's Glimmering Resolution

Upon the hill, a lantern glows,
Its light a beacon, softly shows.
Through storms and shadows, it will stand,
A glimmering hope in a weary land.

With flickering flames, the night recedes,
As dreams awaken, heart's true seeds.
The whispers of the past unite,
In resolution's warming light.

Each flicker tells of journeys fought,
Of battles lost, of wisdom sought.
In every glow, resilience lies,
To open hearts and open skies.

The lantern's dance, a guiding way,
Through darkened nights, it won't betray.
In silence, it will gently flow,
A radiant truth, forever aglow.

So follow close, let shadows fade,
With lantern's light, be unafraid.
For in its glow, your path will find,
A glimmering resolution, kind.

The Dance of Elan and Enchantment

In twilight's grace, they twirl and sway,
Whispers soft, guiding the way.
Elan's spirit, vibrant and bright,
Enchantment weaves through the night.

Laughter echoes, as stars align,
Steps in rhythm, a thread divine.
Magic lingers in the air,
Melodies spun beyond compare.

Glowing orbs in a cosmic stream,
Timeless waltz, like a dream.
Hearts entwined in sweet embrace,
Lost in the dance, a sacred space.

Every twirl, a spark of fate,
Underneath the moon, they create.
In each glance, a tale unfolds,
A dance of love, forever bold.

As dawn's light begins to break,
The rhythm softens, but hearts awake.
In the quiet, they find peace,
From the dance, their souls release.

Fables Carved in Ethereal Light

Once upon a time, stones would speak,
Echoing dreams, unique and meek.
Each fable found in shadowed glens,
Stories whispered by ancient friends.

Moonlit tales of love and loss,
Carved in whispers, never gloss.
Light reveals the hidden paths,
Guiding souls through aftermaths.

A forest deep, where secrets dwell,
Laughter lingers, like a spell.
In every breeze, a story shared,
The magic lives, forever bared.

From olden times, the lessons trace,
In every heart, a sacred space.
Ethereal glow of twilight's grace,
Binds us all in time and place.

Brothers, sisters, tales unite,
Fables carved in ethereal light.
So listen close, let spirits guide,
In every tale, our truths abide.

Hues of Mysticism at Dawn's Edge

Softly waking, the world ablaze,
Mystical hues, in morning's gaze.
Golden strands in the sky's embrace,
Dancing light fills every space.

Whispers of dawn, sweetly unfold,
Stories hidden in the gold.
Nature stirs in gentle song,
Awakening where dreams belong.

The edge of night, a canvas bright,
Splashing colors, pure delight.
Each hue a tale, each shade a sigh,
Mysticism paints the waking sky.

In shadows deep, daybreak weaves,
Promises born on morning leaves.
Moments captured in fleeting light,
Painting visions, warm and bright.

As daybreak blooms, the spirit lifts,
Mystic beauty in nature's gifts.
At dawn's edge, where magic lies,
New beginnings under the skies.

Flickering Hopes Under Moonlit Skies

Under the glow of a silver moon,
Hopes flicker softly, like a tune.
Whispers travel on the night breeze,
Carrying dreams with gentle ease.

Stars above in a velvet sea,
Each one a wish, longing to be.
Hearts alight with the promise held,
In the quiet, stories swelled.

Flickering flames in a place so dear,
Every spark whispers what we fear.
Yet in darkness, we find our way,
Embracing night, welcoming day.

Through the shadows, we wander bold,
Flickering hopes, a tale retold.
Beneath the moon's watchful eye,
Possibilities begin to fly.

So let your heart take flight tonight,
Under the glow, in pure delight.
Flickering hopes, a guiding star,
Leading us gently, wherever we are.

Chronicles from the Mystic Brook

Beneath the whispering willows' shade,
A brook flows softly, secrets laid.
Ripples dance to an unseen tune,
Reflecting tales of sun and moon.

The stones remember each story told,
Of love, of loss, of hearts of gold.
Gentle breezes carry the words,
Like tender songs sung by the birds.

Night wraps the brook in silken dark,
Stars peek down, a celestial spark.
Mystic waters, whisper and sigh,
Guarding dreams as the night drifts by.

Time wanders lightly, traces the past,
Each moment cherished, forever cast.
The brook runs on, a timeless friend,
In its embrace, all sorrows mend.

Glimmers of twilight, shadows converge,
Memories linger, softly emerge.
Chronicles flow in a silver stream,
Hold tight the whispers, dance with the dream.

Dreams Cast in Sapphire Haze

In the twilight where shadows blend,
Dreams take flight, their colors mend.
Sapphire haze wraps the earth in glow,
Whispers of secrets only they know.

Underneath the endless sky so wide,
Imagination's horse begins to ride.
Waves of azure, casting their spell,
Carrying hearts where visions dwell.

Stars like diamonds in velvet space,
Guide the wanderers lost in grace.
Every heartbeat is a thousand tales,
On the breeze, the soft night exhales.

From the depths of slumber's embrace,
Dreams emerge with a gentle pace.
They linger lightly, then fade away,
Leaving traces of night in the day.

In quiet corners of the mind,
Infinite wonders are intertwined.
Sapphire visions, elusive, bright,
Chase the shadows, embrace the light.

Tapestries Woven of Starshine

In the silence of cosmic embrace,
Tapestries shimmer, woven with grace.
Threads of starlight, glimmering bright,
Crafting the fabric of endless night.

Dreams and wishes entwined with care,
Each stitch a story, bold yet rare.
Galaxies dance in the weave of fate,
Time and space contemplate, await.

Whispers of comets and echoes of moons,
Filled with the music of ancient tunes.
Patterns emerging like thoughts in air,
Unraveling tales only night can share.

In the realm where the heart finds peace,
Mysteries flow, and sorrows cease.
Tapestries glisten, alive with delight,
Woven in moments, kissed by starlight.

As dawn approaches, they start to fade,
Yet in our hearts, the memories laid.
For each constellation holds a dream,
A tapestry spun of light's soft gleam.

Riddles Amongst Fallen Leaves

In autumn's grasp, where whispers lie,
Fallen leaves dance and drift, they sigh.
Crimson and gold, a blanket spread,
Stories of seasons, in silence, tread.

Beneath the boughs, secrets reside,
Riddles linger where shadows hide.
Each crinkle and crackle, a tale unfolds,
Of moments cherished and hearts of gold.

Winds carry laughter, a child's delight,
As leaves swirl softly, catching light.
Nature speaks in cryptic tones,
In every rustle, a truth atones.

The paths we wander, entwined with fate,
Echo the whispers, never too late.
Amongst the leaves, the past will weave,
Riddles await as we dare to believe.

So pause a moment, breathe it all in,
Find the riddles where stories begin.
In the dance of the leaves, embrace the lore,
For nature's riddles open every door.

Mystical Currents in Silence

Whispers dance in twilight's grasp,
Shadows weave through ancient trees,
A place where secrets softly clasp,
In stillness, hearts find quiet ease.

Moonlight spills on water's form,
Ripples hold the night's embrace,
Nature breathes in secret storm,
And dreams ignite in hidden space.

Vibrations hum beneath the boughs,
Echoes call from distant shores,
The air is thick with timeless vows,
As wonder opens ancient doors.

In silence deep, a current sways,
Its song an unbroken thread,
We drift where light and shadow plays,
Awash in visions softly spread.

So let us float on silent streams,
Where every heartbeat finds its way,
In mystical currents, our dreams,
We'll dance until the break of day.

Glade of the Waker's Dawn

In the glade where morning glows,
Awakening with gentle grace,
Sunrise paints the world in prose,
Each shadow finds its rightful place.

Birdsong flutters through the air,
A melody of life reborn,
Nature stirs without a care,
From slumber's kiss, the day is torn.

Dewdrops shimmer on the leaves,
Reflecting hopes of journeys new,
In this grove, the heart believes,
That magic still can bloom and brew.

Gentle breezes tease the grass,
With whispers soft of what could be,
In this glade, each moment glass,
Holds potential, wild and free.

So linger here, let worries fade,
As sunlight crowns the waking dawn,
In the glade, our dreams are made,
As life unfolds with every yawn.

A Tuning Fork of Dreams and Enchantment

In twilight's hush, the air is spun,
A tuning fork that strikes the night,
Resonating with the sun,
Enchantment blooms in soft twilight.

Whispers of the stars align,
Each note unfolds a hidden tale,
The universe is yours and mine,
As dreams like fragrant breezes sail.

With every chime, the heartless weep,
A melody of lost design,
Yet hope is woven in the deep,
Where dreams and waking worlds entwine.

In shadows cast by moonlit beams,
We wander through dappled streams,
A sacred space where silence gleams,
And every moment gently seems.

So strike the fork, let echoes soar,
For in this music, find our place,
In dreams and enchantment evermore,
We'll dance with time in a tender grace.

Secrets Flowing Through Starlit Rivers

Beneath the skies where starlight drips,
A river flows with tales untold,
It lulls the mind with gentle sips,
Of secrets wrapped in twilight's fold.

The water shimmers, a silver thread,
Carrying whispers of the past,
Each ripple cradles dreams once said,
As time, like currents, flows steadfast.

Among the banks where shadows play,
And soft reflections greet the night,
The heartbeat of the world in sway,
Reveals the magic in its flight.

Glimmers dance where silence dwells,
In echoes of the night's embrace,
A tapestry of ancient spells,
Spun in the river's secret space.

So listen close, the starlit streams,
They share the wonders of the night,
For in their flow, we find our dreams,
And dance in cosmic, pure delight.

www.ingramcontent.com/pod-product-compliance
Ingram Content Group UK Ltd.
Pitfield, Milton Keynes, MK11 3LW, UK
UKHW021445210125
4208UKWH00003B/118

9 781805 592495